Opposites Attract

Written by Laura Baker

Illustrated by Diego Vaisberg

This is Magnet Dot. Dot lives in a red house with a blue roof.

That is Magnet Tod. Tod lives in a blue house with a red roof.

Dot lives on the left, and Tod lives on the right.

Dot and Tod do **not** get along. They repulse each other.
In fact, they **repel** each other. Truly.

Whenever they get close, they **push** each other away.
Dot goes one way, and Tod goes the other.

They are much too
different to be friends.

Dot loves to collect things from all around town.

She drags rocks to her collection, and feathers, and twigs.

But when she can use her magnetism, that's even better. She has
only to go near some metal things, and she can **pull** them to her.

Pointy things

and pretty things,

zooming things

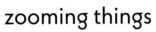

and booming things.

Tod collects things, too:

key rings

and spinning things,

tiny tins

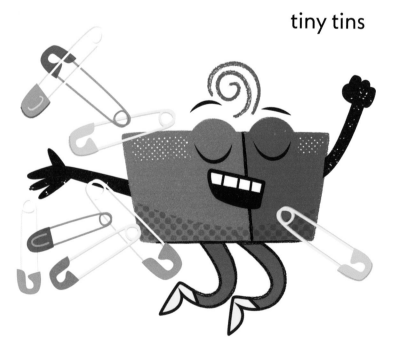

and shiny pins ...

... anything that sticks!

One day, Tod sees the most amazing magnetic thing **ever** –

but Dot has seen it as well.

THUNK! THUNK!

Dot and Tod hold on tight.

Dot's south pole sticks to the thing's north pole, and Tod's north pole sticks to the thing's south pole.

"It's mine!" says Dot.

"I saw it first!" says Tod.

They **pull** with equal strength, and neither Tod nor Dot will let go.

9

Then, suddenly, the thing wakes up!

"Hey!" it says.

It **wiggles** a little, **wriggles** a little, and then slides itself free and walks away.

Suddenly, the force of their opposite poles **attracting** is so strong that Dot and Tod are **pulled** together, south pole to north pole.

THUNK!

Dot is stuck to Tod, and Tod is stuck to Dot.

"Let go of me!" they say together.
"I was out collecting, and you've ruined it!"

"Wait ..." says Tod, slowly. "You like collecting things?"

"I LOVE collecting things," says Dot.

"Me too," says Tod.

Dot and Tod are silent for a moment.

"Wait!" says Tod again, suddenly.
"We're not **repelling** each other!"

Dot smiles slowly. Then she grins.

"Stick with me," she says. "I'll show you some
amazing things I've found."

Dot and Tod walk home together. Dot tells Tod all about her collection as they walk.

"Just wait until you see my toy train!" she says.

Tod tells Dot about the things he's collected, too.

"You won't believe my toy plane!" he says.

They see now that they are as much the same as they are different.

But it doesn't actually matter.

It turns out that opposites **attract**, anyway!

Published by Pearson Education Limited, 80 Strand, London, WC2R 0RL.

www.pearsonschools.co.uk

Text © Pearson Education Limited 2020

Written by Laura Baker

Project managed and edited Just Content Limited

Original illustrations © Pearson Education Limited 2020

Illustrated by Diego Vaisberg

Designed and typeset by Collaborate Agency Limited

First published 2020

23 22 21 20

10 9 8 7 6 5 4 3 2 1

British Library Cataloguing in Publication Data

A catalogue record for this book is available from the British Library

ISBN 978 0 435 20147 0

Printed in Slovakia by Neografia

Note from the publisher

Pearson has robust editorial processes, including answer and fact checks, to ensure the accuracy of the content in this publication, and every effort is made to ensure this publication is free of errors. We are, however, only human, and occasionally errors do occur. Pearson is not liable for any misunderstandings that arise as a result of errors in this publication, but it is our priority to ensure that the content is accurate. If you spot an error, please do contact us at resourcescorrections@pearson.com so we can make sure it is corrected.